Original title:
The Orchard's Crown

Copyright © 2025 Creative Arts Management OÜ
All rights reserved.

Author: Wyatt Kensington
ISBN HARDBACK: 978-1-80586-444-8
ISBN PAPERBACK: 978-1-80586-916-0

## Melody of the Vines

In the garden where grapes swing,
The squirrels tap dance, what a thing!
A cat in shades, a cool meow,
Sipping the sun, oh take a bow.

Bumbling bees buzz high and low,
With every sip, they steal the show.
A gnome on guard, what a sight,
Waving his hat from left to right.

**Festooned with Abundance**

Cherry pies up in the trees,
Chasing birds with sticky knees.
Winks and giggles all around,
Joyful chaos here is found.

Lemons rolling like a ball,
Laughter echoes through it all.
With every pluck, a funny face,
Fruit on a mission, keeping pace.

## The Embrace of Soil

Worms do wiggles, oh so slick,
While daisies giggle with a kick.
Sunshine tickles every sprout,
Nature's party is about.

Strawberries play hide and seek,
With whispers bright, they make us squeak.
A rabbit hops, forgot his cue,
Too busy munching on a shoe!

## An Interlude in Green

Fennel frolics, carrots cheer,
"Don't eat me!" they squeal in fear.
Tomatoes blush beneath the sun,
Shy and juicy, having fun.

Onions grinning from the patch,
Stirring up a clever batch.
Soil and sunshine, what a dream,
In this garden, laughs just gleam.

## Nectar of the Earth

Bumblebees buzz with delight,
Taking nectar, what a sight!
Their little dance, a funny show,
As they bumble to and fro.

Fruit hanging low, ripe for the bite,
Squirrels plotting, ready to fight.
Chasing shadows, they leap and dart,
A nutty race, a furry art!

**Shadows Among the Apple Trees**

Underneath the leafy shade,
A picnic spread, laughter played.
Someone's sandwich flies away,
A hovering bird steals the display!

The shadows dance, a playful sight,
With giggles echoing in the light.
A squirrel watches, quite bemused,
As humans feast, their snacks abused!

## The Song of Ripening

Blossoms twirl in breezy curls,
Each petal tells of juicy whirls.
A hoe starts humming its own tune,
As if to woo the laughing moon.

With every fruit, a joke is born,
Like apples grinning, oh so worn.
Gardener giggles, tripping near,
He finds a banana, "Not my sphere!"

## Echoes of the Orchard

In the orchard, whispers spread,
Of funny tales and laughter bred.
A chicken struts, a crown on head,
"Am I royalty?" it proudly said!

The echoes bounce between the trees,
Tickling fancies in the breeze.
Every twist and turn brings glee,
Nature's laughter, wild and free!

## Lyrical Roots

In a grove where fruit trees sway,
Lemons giggle, apples play.
Orange jokes on peachy days,
Nature's humor in bright arrays.

Birds in ties, they chirp and dance,
Squirrels wearing hats, they prance.
Every branch a song, a chance,
To laugh beneath leaves' wild romance.

## Poetry Among the Blossoms

Pollen poets buzz around,
Writing verses on the ground.
Bees debate, their hum profound,
In floral worlds where joy is found.

Petal confetti in the breeze,
Daisies dancing with such ease.
Lilies laugh as bumblebees,
Share their tales with cheeky tease.

## The Heart of Nature's Choir

In the chorus of the trees,
Frogs hit high notes, singing keys.
Chipmunks clap with great expertise,
As nature's laughter floats with ease.

Wind whips through in flirty tones,
Whistling secrets through the stones.
Caterpillars on their phones,
Texting jokes to their friend, the drones.

## **Essence of Blooming**

Blossoms wink in colors bright,
Jokes unfold at morning light.
Fruitcake trees prepare for night,
With frosting clouds, a silly sight.

Giggles rustle through the grass,
Sunflowers striking poses, class.
Nature's fun, it will not pass,
As laughter echoes, none to harass.

## The Language of Trees

In whispers soft, the branches sway,
They gossip more than kids at play.
The apples blush, they can't conceal,
The juicy secrets they reveal.

A pear declared, quite proud and round,
"I'm the juiciest in town!"
But lemon laughed, with zestful glee,
"You're sweet, but I'm the life of spree!"

The cherry trees, all dressed in pink,
Conspired hard over lemonade drink.
They giggle low, and plot at dusk,
A fruit parade, for fun, a must!

So if you stroll where shadows loom,
Prepare to join the fruit festoon.
Where trees exchange their funny tales,
And laughter dances on the gales.

**Tales from the Canopy**

Up in the trees, where squirrels prance,
Is where the fruit do a silly dance.
Banana slips, and wiggles down,
Leaves the others giggling in a frown.

A grape once told, in juicy tones,
"I've got the best bunch of funny bones!"
But kiwi said, with fuzzy might,
"I'll take your grapes and turn 'em bright!"

The branches shook with merry sound,
As laughter echoed all around.
Each fruit had tales, of dreams and schemes,
In the canopy where fun redeems!

So climb a tree, hear their delight,
Join the fruit chatter, day or night.
You'll find the laughter, pure and true,
In the canopy, where friends renew.

## Twilight's Fruit-Tree Serenade

As twilight glows, the trees get chatty,
With jokes that make the crickets happy.
An orange winked, with zest and flair,
"I'm the brightest one, do you dare?"

The raspberry said, with seedy grins,
"Sweetness isn't all, it's how one spins!"
While apples hung, with rosy pride,
"We are the treat that can't be denied!"

The lemons sang in sour tones,
"Life's zesty, with all its moans!"
While laughing pears rolled side to side,
In this twilight, they won't hide.

So join the dance, on branches wide,
Where fruits are friends and giggles abide.
In twilight's glow, the trees will hum,
A serenade for anyone to come.

## **Embers of Forgotten Seasons**

Amidst the leaves, old tales ignite,
Of fruits that glowed in the golden light.
The fig once bragged, with grand esteem,
"I was the king of every dream!"

But oak tree laughed, with sturdy bark,
"You're just a snack in my park!"
The coconut chimed, from high above,
"I'm a hard nut, but full of love!"

While winter trees, with branches bare,
Spun stories of warmth, a fruity affair.
They laughed of summers, long ago,
When they were young, and their hearts aglow!

So gather 'round, for seasons' end,
And listen close, let nature send.
The funny tales of fruit and trees,
In the embers of time, we find our ease.

**Interwoven Destinies**

In a garden where ants march on parade,
A squirrel throws nuts without being afraid.
An apple fell down with a plump, silly thud,
While a rabbit nearby just rolled in the mud.

The trees gossip loudly in leaf-laden tones,
As the wind tells the roots all their secret bones.
An owl hoots at night, saying, "Who's got the cheese?"
While the hedgehog just wriggles, all covered in leaves.

## The Retreat of Nature's Hand

A frog sings a tune with a quack and a croak,
While the flowers all giggle at the shape of the oak.
A beetle digs deep in a soil so divine,
Wearing sunglasses, complaining, "Where's my wine?"

The daisies dance wildly, in colorful rows,
While the daisies yell out, "Stop stepping on toes!"
A cow joins the party, mooing joyfully loud,
Claiming it's the best fun she's ever had, proud.

**In the Shadow of Arboreal Splendor**

Beneath leafy giants, a snail makes a trek,
With a sign that says, "Next rest stop: a wreck!"
A chipmunk in shades scopes the scene from a bough,
Leaving the audience saying, "What's he doing now?"

The flowers all chuckle, as bees buzz about,
Some dreaming of honey, others plotting a pout.
A tortoise jogs by, exclaiming, "What a sprint!"
As the elder trees cheer, though they think he might glint.

## Dappled Light and Silent Whispers

The sunbeams are tickling the tips of the leaves,
While some snails are plotting for mischief, it seems.
A parrot in bloom, full of colors and flair,
Tells jokes to the branches; they giggle, beware!

In the berry patch, a fox wears a hat,
Complaining of pollen, then sneezing—just splat!
The figs roll their eyes, oh the drama, no doubt,
As the laughter erupts in this wild, fruity shout!

**Blooms Amidst the Shadows**

In a patch where sunflowers grin,
The apples yell, "Let the games begin!"
A squirrel stole a pie with flair,
Hiding it under the teddy bear.

Hasty bees in comical flight,
Try to dance but lose their sight.
A cucumber rolled down the way,
Declared it was now salad day!

Blushing tomatoes join the fun,
So many giggles, we cannot run.
The moon winks from the leafy shroud,
Laughing at the mischief loud.

Whispers tickle the cherry trees,
As laughter floats upon the breeze.
Fruits chuckle, sharing their dreams,
In the orchard of playful themes.

## **Beneath the Tree's Canopy**

Beneath the branches, shadows play,
A beetle claims he's king today.
Nuts gossip of the wind's wild game,
While pears brag about their fame.

A mouse in a hat, so very dapper,
Sings karaoke with a happy crapper.
Kites swoop down, to steal the cheese,
But the tree just chuckles in the breeze.

A banana slipped on a blueberry,
And proclaimed it was quite scary!
The breeze tickles the cheeks of grass,
As daisies giggle, "This too shall pass!"

With laughter ripe and joy profound,
Every critter dances round.
Beneath the canopy up high,
The orchard sings a playful sigh.

## Fables of the Ripened Harvest

Once an apple thought it wise,
To tell a tale that made fruit cry.
A carrot dressed up as a queen,
Told tales of veggies so unseen.

The pumpkins laughed, their cheeks so round,
At tricks that grew up from the ground.
A cabbage tried to tell a joke,
But choked on laughter, what a bloke!

The cornflakes sang with crispy glee,
While beets spun tales of great decree.
"Don't pull my roots!" they squealed with cheer,
As rhymes danced about from ear to ear.

With every word, the fruits would beam,
Creating wacky fables, a dream.
Who knew harvests could be this fun,
In the orchard's laughter, we all run!

## The Dance of Blossoms and Bees

In the garden where daisies trip,
Blossoms giggle in a silly zip.
Bees don hats and twirl their wings,
Buzzing tunes that make hearts sing.

A daffodil slipped on a bee,
"Don't mind me, I'm just full of glee!"
The tulips twirled in polka dots,
As snails laughed at those clumsy thoughts.

With pollen sprinkled like confetti,
They danced and spun, feeling all setty.
Cherries whispered, "Join the spree!"
As colors burst, wild and free.

With every spin, the joy increased,
Nature's party was a feast.
The dance of color, cheer, and ease,
Brought all to laugh, oh, what a tease!

## Nature's Quiet Contemplation

In the shade, a squirrel dances,
Chasing dreams, not second glances.
The bees conduct their buzzing band,
While flowers giggle, hand in hand.

A rabbit munches with delight,
Munching greens from morn till night.
A snail races with a leaf,
Claiming speed, but in disbelief.

The sunlight tickles boughs so bright,
Creating shadows full of light.
Each tree whispers secrets fair,
With laughter echoing in the air.

A caterpillar writes a book,
On life and leaves, with quite the look.
The world seems silly in this place,
Nature's giggles put on a face.

## The Pulse of the Earth

Roots tap dance beneath the ground,
With rhythms only worms have found.
Beetles groove in quiet style,
While ivy climbs, it takes a while.

The sun breaks in with a bright grin,
While critters play, let the games begin!
A fox winks at a startled hare,
Says, 'Join me, friend, there's fun to share!'

Clouds flirt and tease the trees above,
As thunder rolls, it fits like a glove.
Raindrops drum on leaves with flair,
Making melodies that fill the air.

Earth giggles softly, can you hear?
With each pulse, it brings us cheer.
Each breeze a chuckle, soft and spry,
Nature's laughter up to the sky.

## A Realm of Trees

In this realm where branches play,
Pinecones fall, a game of ballet.
The trees tell stories, oh so grand,
Of acorns dressed in grassy bands.

A woodpecker drums a silly song,
While vines twist around, not wanting to be wrong.
Chipmunks hoard their treasures tight,
In a stand-off, hilarious sight!

Leaves play tag with the gentle breeze,
While shadows dance between the trees.
Barking dogs join in the fun,
As sunlight chases everyone.

Nature's courts, where laughter's king,
With every twist, a new fling.
In this kingdom of green delight,
The trees wear crowns, oh what a sight!

## Odyssey of Saplings

Tiny saplings stretch with glee,
Pretending they're as tall as can be.
In the wind, they sway and bend,
Whispering secrets, 'Let's not pretend!'

A dance-off starts with ferns galore,
As mushrooms cheer and clamor for more.
The sun offers snacks, warm and sweet,
While twigs tap out a steady beat.

A brave little sprout makes a cheer,
As clouds roll in, they play near.
Nature's children in their prime,
Giggle and jostle, it's sapling time!

In this journey, small but bold,
Every moment a joy to behold.
Together they grow, laugh, and play,
In the odyssey of green every day.

# Meditations Under the Sky

Beneath the branches, squirrels prance,
They chatter, dance, a wild romance.
I sip my drink, they steal my snack,
Who knew that nature had such a knack?

A crow drops down with a cheeky caw,
Stealing ideas straight from my jaw.
I ponder life with lemonade flair,
While bees debate who finds the best pair.

The sun plays hide and seek all day,
While shadows tell jokes in a silly way.
I laugh out loud, the squirrels pause,
Wondering if I'm quite the cause.

With fruit so ripe, I take a bite,
And every sweet taste feels just right.
But who knew grapes could hold a grudge,
When they bubble up and give a nudge?

## The Canvas of Falling Leaves

Leaves tumble down in a golden swirl,
As I trip over them, my toes unfurl.
A red one lands on my chair with flair,
It seems to say, 'You should take care!'

Each leaf a dancer, twirling in air,
Whispering secrets with a hint of dare.
I laugh as they paint my head in red,
Who knew being clumsy could be widespread?

Squirrels play tag while I sit and shout,
'You've won the game, there's no doubt!'
They gather up nuts as I gather dreams,
In a world of giggles and silly themes.

The sun warms the day with a playful grin,
While shadows behind me try to fit in.
I wink at them and give a shout,
'Join the fun, there's no need to pout!'

## **Echoes of Fragrance**

In the garden blooms a flower bright,
Its scent so sweet, it takes to flight.
I sneeze and cough, what a fuss,
Is it the petals or just me that's thus?

Honeybees buzz, they're buzzing mad,
Grabbing a sip, getting quite glad.
They dance on petals like they're in a race,
I stumble around, keeping up the pace.

The roses whisper stories of love,
While daisies giggle from high above.
A wobbly path, I walk with glee,
Who knew that fragrance could tickle me?

With scents that mingle, a funny sight,
Pollen's a party, oh what delight!
But here comes a sneeze, it's taking copious rounds,
'The garden's too cheery, let's quit the sounds!'.

## Reflections on the Breeze

The wind's a joker with playful hands,
It tickles noses, and ruffles strands.
I chase my hat as it laughs away,
'You think you can catch me? Not today!'

The sun winks up with a bright surprise,
As kites take flight in endless skies.
I join the fun with a gleeful spin,
But who's the master of the windy din?

Leaves do the conga, twirling on high,
I'm just a spectator, waving goodbye.
While clouds puff up like marshmallow treats,
Nature's comedy never skips beats.

So here's to the breeze, with laughter in tow,
It lifts our spirits, so go with the flow.
Let's dance with the wind, sing out loud,
In the joyful chaos, let's be proud!

## Celestial Harvest

In the tree, a squirrel dances,
With acorns as his funny pants.
He gathers nuts like no tomorrow,
While birds just watch and laugh in sorrow.

A plump raccoon joins the fray,
Snagging pears in a cheeky way.
His sticky paws get stuck in jam,
Oh, what a sight—he's quite the ham!

Bees buzz round with a silly tune,
Wearing hats shaped like the moon.
They bump and swirl in the sweet delight,
While ants march on in tiny fright.

At sunset's glow, they all convene,
To share the spoils of the seen.
With giggles echoing through the night,
They celebrate under stars so bright.

## Moments in the Glade

In the glade, the frogs proclaim,
That jumping high is all their game.
With splashes loud, the lily pads quack,
While crickets laugh at the frog's back.

A hedgehog rolls in clumps of leaves,
Pretending he's lost his sharpest cleaves.
His friends all giggle at his plight,
"Come back, dear spiny, you're quite a sight!"

The rabbits race, a raucous scene,
Bouncing round, they're oh so keen.
Tripping over roots with all their might,
They tumble down, what a silly sight!

Under trees, the shadows play,
While the sunbeams chase the clouds away.
Nature's laughter fills the space,
In this glade of joy, a happy place.

## A Stillness Among the Blooms


In a garden of blooms, all so bright,
A sleepy bee dreams of flight.
With nectar sips, he's in a haze,
Buzzing soft in the sunlight's rays.

A butterfly dances, but trips on a leaf,
Landing near, with a comic relief.
It wriggles up, with grace gone askew,
All the flowers chuckle, who knew?

Ladybugs gather for a tea,
Sipping dew drops with glee.
They gossip 'bout the latest trends,
Like who has spots and who pretends.

With petals swirling in the breeze,
Nature's giggle flows with ease.
In this garden, joy's the rule,
Funny critters play, oh, how cool!

## Lullabies of the Wild

By the brook, a raccoon hums,
Sharing tales of silly thumbs.
His friends all howl in pure delight,
With laughter echoing through the night.

In the trees, owls share a wink,
As fireflies gather, all in sync.
They dance and twirl in the cool twilight,
A glimmering joke in the fading light.

A fox struts by with a fancy hat,
Saying, "Every critter needs a spat!"
Squirrels giggle, "Not like that, dear friend,
Your style's a mess, it's time to mend!"

With the stars twinkling as their guide,
All creatures gather, side by side.
In the wild, where laughter's the sound,
They sing their lullabies, joyfully crowned.

## **Wandering Through the Glade**

In the glade where giggles bloom,
Squirrels dance and apples loom.
A bee who thinks it's quite the knight,
Buzzes loudly, a silly flight.

Frogs wear hats of lily pads,
Playing hopscotch, oh my, such fads!
A rabbit hops and makes a bet,
On who can eat the most – you bet!

The trees are whispering quite a joke,
About a mischievous old oak.
Who tried to sneak a swing at noon,
But missed and tripped, oh what a swoon!

With laughter echoing all around,
The glade is where pure joy is found.
So join the fun, don't be shy,
In the silly dance beneath the sky!

## Sunlight and Shadows

Sunlight pours like honey thick,
While shadows play their silly trick.
A dancing leaf, oh what a sight,
It swirled and twirled in pure delight.

A babbling brook, it slips and slides,
Inviting fish with silly strides.
They wear tiny hats, a fishy gag,
Swimming past with a cheeky brag.

Little birds with voices bold,
Can't stop singing tales of gold.
About the day the sun went green,
Chasing shadows like a scene!

Through sunlight bright and shadows long,
Laughter rings, a joyful song.
Join the fun beneath the trees,
Where silly antics flow like breeze!

## Threads of Time and Life

In the tapestry of days gone by,
A squirrel stitches with a sigh.
He drops his thread, it starts to fray,
And knits a sweater made of hay!

Time is twisted, quite absurd,
With frogs who think they're still a bird.
They croak their plans to take a flight,
But sit on lily pads, what a sight!

A fox claims to have time-warped news,
That tomorrow brings an apple cruise.
But ending up at cheese instead,
He laughs it off and shakes his head.

Threads of life weave tales so grand,
Where jesters play in this fine land.
So gather 'round, don't miss the fun,
In the fabric of time, we're all one!

## Savoring the Harvest

In the patch where pumpkins grin wide,
And tomatoes roll in gleeful pride.
They play a game of hide and seek,
With silly shadows, oh so cheek!

Carrots dance in their orange hue,
While radishes wear hats that grew.
Potatoes joke with roots beneath,
In a quirky harvest, no one's sheathe!

The basket's full, yet one slipped out,
It's racing round, it's in a rout!
Chasing crows who've come to snatch,
The funniest game of higgledy hatch!

So savor laughs and tasty cheer,
In the harvest, joy is near.
Let's feast on stories shared in mirth,
As nature's clowns reveal their worth!

# A Tapestry of Leaf and Sun

In the shade of trees, squirrels dare,
They chase each other, without a care.
Apples giggle, ripe for the bite,
Pigeons doze off, dreaming of flight.

Breezes tease branches, a ticklish spree,
Lemonade whispers, 'Come play with me!'
Dancing around, the ants throw a ball,
While bees are buzzing, they're having a ball.

With laughter aplenty and shadows so sweet,
Every round fruit thinks it's a treat.
The sun spills laughter, olive green,
In this jolly orchard, it's all quite a scene!

So come take a stroll, feel the mirth,
Among twinkling leaves, let joy burst.
With smiles like sunshine, find giggles aplenty,
In this merry grove that feels oh-so-gretty!

## **The Hidden Harvest**

Underneath leaves, treasures appear,
Fruits hold secrets, take a peek here!
Grapes wear capes, prancing with flair,
While pumpkins hide, in their orange lair.

Rabbits plot mischief and plan their pranks,
While cherries laugh, forming fruit ranks.
The carrots conjure, hopscotch delight,
As veggies engage in a playful fight.

Beneath sturdy branches, the fun never wanes,
Berries throw parties, with no need for chains.
With dancing radishes, in vibrant dress,
Ripe cucumbers aim for a humorous mess!

So join the laughter, don't lag behind,
In this silly harvest, all joy you'll find.
For every fruit bears a joke to give,
Hidden in gardens, where laughter can live!

## **Treasures of the Glistening Grove**

In the glistening grove, treasures do gleam,
Fruits are quirky, bursting with dream.
Pineapples giggle, swinging in glee,
While pears share tales, quite fruity and free.

Figs in their jackets, all fancy and proud,
Invite the squirrels to sing out loud.
Avocados roll, in a slippery game,
As berries challenge, for fruitiest fame.

Peaches held secret, unfolding their charm,
While plums play tag, causing no harm.
Each nutty acorn tries to impress,
With silly jokes in a leafy dress.

So dance with the wind, in this jovial spot,
Where laughter's the treasure, melting the plot.
Under the canopy, join this wild fray,
In the glistening grove, let's frolic and play!

## A Symphony of Blossoms

Petals are prancing, a colorful show,
Winds conduct laughter, as blossoms do glow.
Bees hum their tunes, oh what a sound,
Fluttering melodies all around!

The daisies twirl in whimsical glee,
While tulips chat, 'Oh look at me!'
Lilies wear hats, with flowers so bright,
In this symphony, each color takes flight.

Sunflowers grin, towering so tall,
'We're the stars of the show, after all!'
As violets giggle and dance in the air,
The blooms orchestrate joy, beyond compare.

So come join the symphony, let spirits rise,
With laughter and blossoms, under sunny skies.
Among these choral notes of vibrant cheer,
Life's a funny song, whenever you're near!

## **Petals Beneath the Stars**

Under a sky where workers dream,
A raccoon steals the fruit's good cream.
The apples giggle, their cheeks so red,
While pumpkins whisper, 'We're overfed!'

The moon's a peach on a silver plate,
While fireflies dance and don't appreciate.
Trees sway jolly as they tickle the night,
Birds laugh at shadows, what a funny sight!

A squirrel in socks scurries with glee,
Mocking the cat who's stuck in a tree.
A thunderous giggle echoes in the breeze,
Nature's punchline, aiming to please!

So under these stars, mischief unfolds,
In fruity delight, the story is told.
With petals like feathers, the world's made of cheer,
Laughter and joy—now let's raise a beer!

## **Branches of Memory**

In the orchard of thoughts, what a sight we keep,
Where memories dangle like fruit on a sheep.
A cherry tree thinks it's far too cool,
While the elderberry plays the clownish fool.

The shadows of laughter dance overhead,
Tickled by whispers of stories long dead.
The figs are gossiping, oh what a show,
As oranges roll by in their splendid glow!

Now, a cinnamon coffee plant takes a chance,
Biding its time for a wild tree dance.
The branches all sway in rhythmic delight,
While the stars look down, giggling all night.

With sapling dreams and a twisty jest,
The branches remember their very best.
Each leaf a reminder of fun we have met,
While nature's laughter, we'll never forget!

## The Orchard's Embrace

Under twisted vines, mischief thrives,
Where peaches plot and the plum tree arrives.
"I'm juicier than you," bellows the pear,
"Let's have a race, if you dare!"

With taffy winds and a lemon parade,
The nuts are all scheming, genius displayed.
Cherries burst out in a cheer so spry,
"Catch me if you can, I'm the pie in the sky!"

The juice drips down as laughter fills air,
Each fruit sporting smiles that they want to share.
Round the sweet nectar, the bees do sway,
Belly laughs buzzing throughout the play!

From the silly blooms to the roots of fun,
The embrace of mischief makes days feel like sun.
With every juiced joke that these trees can teach,
Life's canvas of laughter is within our reach!

## Palette of the Seasons

Autumn leaf dances on a cheerful breeze,
Complaining about sticky sap on its knees.
Winter dressed up, a pear in white fur,
Saying, "Who needs sun? I'm glitzy for sure!"

Spring sprouts tiny laughs with every bud,
While melted snow drops join in a flood.
The colors assemble for the grand charade,
As flowers bloom bright in a jubilant parade!

Summer brings picnics, though ants claim the food,
With watermelon joys, we're all in the mood.
The sunflowers jest, "We reach for the skies,
While watching the butterflies in disguise!"

What a crazy palette, the seasons create,
A canvas of giggles, oh isn't it great?
With laughter interlaced through the passing times,
The orchard bursts forth with whimsical rhymes!

# Fragrance of Autumn's Dust

Leaves dance in the breeze, oh so spry,
Cider spills like gossip, oh my!
Squirrels wear acorns like hats so bold,
Each nut a treasure, a tale to be told.

Pumpkins sport smiles, grinning so wide,
In this funny patch, there's nowhere to hide!
Every harvest moon shines with laughter,
As we dance 'round the fields, ever after.

Goblins and ghosts in the shadows creep,
But we chuckle and chase them, not losing sleep.
With cider in hand and friends all around,
We're the quirkiest crew this season has found!

So gather the stories, let the masks drop,
In this hilarious harvest, let joy never stop!

## Beneath the Canopy of Time

Underneath the branches, we giggle and sway,
Time takes a break, to join in our play.
Birds crack jokes, as they perch and sing,
While squirrels throw acorns, like nature's bling!

Each knot in the wood is a mystery told,
Of the laughter and mischief, so bold!
Sloths in slow motion, like comedians acting,
Bring chuckles and snorts, their timing exacting.

Sunbeams play tag, as shadows turn shy,
In this whimsical realm, spirits fly high.
Every leaf whispers secrets, soft and spry,
"What's the deal with nature? No reasons why!"

So come and join, under the vast blue,
Where time takes a break, just for me and you.

## Heartbeats of Nature

Flowers burst forth in a colorful spree,
Joking with bees, "Hey, buzz over here!"
The frogs hold a concert, barking with cheer,
While crickets all chirp like they're coaching dear!

Trees stretch their arms, reach for the sky,
Sharing old tales with a wink in their eye.
"Remember that storm? We swayed like mad!"
Laughter erupts from the forest, so glad!

Rabbits hop by, sporting a grin,
With antics so silly, they always win.
Nature's own rhythm, infused with delight,
In this funny heartbeat, everything's right!

So laugh with the leaves and play with the winds,
Join the heartbeat of nature, let the fun begin!

## The Weaving of Roots

Under the soil, the gossip goes deep,
Roots intertwine, secrets they keep.
"Did you hear about that tree? So tall and grand!"
"Yeah, but watch out; there's a gopher that's planned!"

In this underground dance, the worms spin and twirl,
Like nature's own ballet, creating a whirl.
Each burrow a story, each twist a delight,
The ground's underbelly is all out of sight!

The fungi join in with their quirky caps,
Making sure no one forgets the laughs and the naps.
With every little push, they rise, oh so spry,
"Who knew the roots could be such a sly?"

So under the surface, where laughter runs loose,
Join the party with roots, in this jocular truce!

## Whispers of Fruiting Branches

In the shade where apples nap,
A squirrel stole a fruity cap.
He danced and twirled in pure delight,
Singing songs of fruit-filled night.

Pears are plotting, so they claim,
To outshine the apples' fame.
But plums just giggle, full of zest,
Declaring everyone the best.

Cherries gossip, juicy tales,
About the wind that blows their sails.
While berries burst in fits of fun,
With tiny laughs, they always run.

So wander here, within this jest,
Where every fruit is dressed the best.
With jellybeans and sunshine laughs,
The orchard's family happily quaffs.

## Beneath Boughs of Gold

Beneath the trees, the shadows prance,
With shadows looking for a chance.
A pumpkin rolled, declared a race,
With carrots tripping, oh disgrace!

Bananas slip, they scandalize,
While oranges toss aside their lies.
Lemons sneer and laugh in glee,
As limes roll by, feeling free.

The harvest moon begins to giggle,
As apples show off, they wiggle.
And every fruit, a jest to share,
In this sweet garden, joy in the air.

So if you stray beneath these trees,
Expect some hilarity with the breeze.
For fun and laughter is the goal,
In this orchard, bravely roll!

## Secrets in the Evening Light

In twilight's glow, the whispers spin,
Where strawberries hide, hoping to win.
A grape rolled out, declared it a feast,
But the cucumbers laughed, they are not ceased.

Peaches prance with peachy crowns,
While noisy radishes wear frowns.
Figs and dates throw a party bash,
As carrots sing in a joyful clash.

The evening light brings silly tales,
Of fruit debates and veggie trails.
A wit contest, who's the best?
In this garden, we jest and jest!

So tune your ears to the night's sweet tune,
Let laughter lift you like a balloon.
For secrets shared 'neath leafy boughs,
Shall sweeten every merry vow.

## Harvest of Forgotten Dreams

In the field of dreams, we gather round,
Where forgotten fruit begins to sound.
A cantaloupe laughs, 'You lost your way!'
While melons join, 'Come out and play!'

Ripe tomatoes jive in a merry spree,
While zucchinis hum a jazzy decree.
The cornfields sway with a rhythmic beat,
While pumpkins giggle, oh, what a treat!

As harvest stars begin to shine,
Each veggie declares, 'This dance is mine!'
A radish slips, but soon regains,
With every tumble, the fun remains.

So take a basket, come join this fun,
In a patch where laughter's never done.
With whispers and giggles, we shall glean,
The harvest of dreams, a laugh-filled scene!

## **Echoes of the Summer's Yield**

In the laughter of bees, they sip,
Fruits wiggling on branches, a funny trip.
Pies dance on windows, a sweet delight,
As squirrels wear hats in the soft twilight.

Jars clink gently, a jam-packed cheer,
The smell of fresh fruit, we all hold dear.
A melon in slippers, it rolls down the lane,
While pears in a party go slightly insane.

Ghosts of past harvests, in quirky arrays,
Whispering secrets of sillier days.
Apricots giggle and tumble with glee,
As laughter drips sweetly from fruit-laden trees.

Oh, how the laughter of summer rings round,
With each silly fruit, the joy is profound.
We dance in the grass, our toes in the dirt,
A festival of flavors, where none of us hurt.

## **Beneath the Gnarled Roots**

Under roots that twist like a wise octopus,
Nature's confessions, we all laugh thus.
Worms in tuxedos have come to debate,
The merits of planting what grows on a plate.

Rabbits wear spectacles, counting their greens,
While hedgehogs argue about pop culture scenes.
The roots roll their eyes, like elders so wise,
While fruits pull pranks, wearing jesters' ties.

Foxes do tango, with mice in a whirl,
Those critters go wild, how they twist and twirl.
Radishes chuckle in their earthy bed,
As mushrooms throw parties, and laughter is spread.

The shadows of roots share the quirkiest tales,
While nature giggles as each creature prevails.
Beneath the old branches, where secrets take flight,
The fun-loving garden shines all through the night.

## Nectar and Twilight's Embrace

Sweet nectar drips from the clouds up high,
While fruit bats gossip and flutter on by.
Dew drops are giggling, catching a breeze,
As they flip-flop softly from leaf to trees.

The evening sun winks with a cheeky grin,
While cucumbers dance at the farm's little spin.
Peaches in pajamas, they do a light jig,
While zany old prunes just wiggle and dig.

Twilight winks softly, casting spells of delight,
The strawberries hum as they twirl in the light.
Mangoes wear crowns, while cherries complain,
About being snacked on, oh, the fruit's fun disdain.

A nest full of laughter, a quirky parade,
As the fruits all unite in a spunky charade.
With nectar and giggles, the twilight shimmers,
As laughter as rich as the juice always glimmers.

## Fruits of the Forgotten Seasons

Once long ago in a garden so grand,
Came fruits who conspired to take a bold stand.
Bananas wore capes, like heroes they'd play,
While limes threw confetti, shouting hooray!

The apples recalled when they missed their big chance,
To dance on the table in a splendid romance.
Peaches with pom-poms cheered loudly and clear,
As apricots tumbled, feeling no fear.

Time-traveling fruits from seasons gone by,
Open a shop where old flavors can fly.
The raspberries giggle, the kiwis throw shade,
At memories lovely that never did fade.

So here in this garden, where laughter is ripe,
The fruits of the past form a whimsical type.
With joy that cascades, as sweet as their sauce,
The forgotten embrace with delight, not loss.

## Guardians of the Grove

In green hats and big shoes, they glide,
The squirrels hold court, with nuts as their guide.
They chuckle and chatter, with no time to waste,
As the trees shake with laughter, a nutty good taste.

With branches a-dancing and roots holding tight,
The mushrooms declare it's a tickling night.
A family of rabbits, all dressed in their best,
Hatch plans for the party, it's nature's wild fest.

Owl on the branch, quite wise with a wink,
Keeps watch over everyone, quick as a blink.
"Don't trip on a root!" he hoots with a grin,
For he knows that the fun is soon about to begin.

So raise up your glasses, let laughter abound,
With cheeky delights in this joyful surround.
For in this grand grove, what mischief we'll sow,
As guardians unite, the fun just won't slow!

## Nature's Tapestry


In fields of color, the blooms like to prance,
With bees buzzing loudly, they join in the dance.
The daisies gossip, oh what do they say?
"Last week, the roses thought they'd win the bouquet!"

Butterflies flutter in shades that astound,
They flit and they giggle, oh what a sound!
The daisies roll over, each tickle a tease,
As nature's bright palette aims to please.

With whispers of leaves and marigolds grinning,
The laughter erupts, as laughter keeps spinning.
"Who will wear who?" asks the vine to the grass,
As the sun shines a spotlight on this merry mass.

With puddles like mirrors reflecting the fun,
The frogs leap in rhythm, they leap one by one.
In nature's fine weave, such giggles abound,
In this tapestry of joy, where life's joys are found!

## Gleams of Butterfly Wings

In gardens so bright where the colors ignite,
The butterflies chuckle, oh what a sight!
They swoop and they swirl, their wings in a whirl,
Over flowers in laughter, they'll twirl and unfurl.

A ladybug whispers, "Did you see that?"
As bees hold a meeting, all dressed in their chat.
"Who's got the nectar? It's quite the debate!"
With giggles and wiggles, they all celebrate.

With a patter of rain, the muddy boots squelch,
As children slip-slide, giving joy a great selch!
The plants snicker softly, with roots all entwined,
With petals all opening, good humor aligned.

So dance with the butterflies, giggling along,
In this garden they've made, where everyone's strong.
In the gleams of their wings, the happiness sings,
A symphony crafted on colorful flings!

## A Dance of Seasons

Spring giggles, with flowers all sprouted in cheer,
While winter just snickers, "I'm still hanging near!"
Summer bursts forward in bright sunny hats,
As autumn's sly whispers unravel like chats.

"Let's swap our costumes!" the seasons agree,
As leaves spin and twirl in a wild jubilee.
With sweaters in summer and shorts in the snow,
Each season competes, for what fun can they show?

The pine trees all chuckle, while dressed up in frost,
While tulips are thinking, "We won't be lost!"
It's a dance of odd choices, so quirky and bright,
Where laughter keeps echoing from morning till night.

So gather your friends and join in the play,
As seasons unite in an unpredictable way.
With whispers and giggles, life makes quite the fuss,
In this joyful ballet—who wouldn't want to rush?

## **Echoing Laughter of Summer**

Beneath the sun, we dance and twirl,
Fruit flies past, a berry swirl.
Giggles blend with rustling leaves,
Nature's jest that never deceives.

Mango, peach, a slippery race,
We dodge the branches, a sweet embrace.
The laughter echoes, loud and clear,
As apples tumble, we cheer and jeer.

Silly hats made of vine and twig,
Wear them proud, it feels so big!
Lemons laugh when falling low,
Squeezed for juice, they steal the show.

In this fruity world, we are the jesters,
Daring bites, our daring testers.
With every chomp, a joke unfurls,
Summer's laughter, a gift that twirls.

## Beneath the Arbor's Shade

Under leafy roofs, we share our dreams,
With shadows dancing in playful beams.
A cheeky squirrel, he joins our game,
Stealing nuts, we laugh at his fame.

Picnic spreads under the laughing sun,
Sandwiches fly—oh, that was fun!
With pickles rolling like merry balls,
We shout and giggle as each one falls.

Juggling oranges, a sunny delight,
One slips and rolls, oh what a sight!
We chase it down, a laugh out loud,
Within this shade, we feel so proud.

So here we sit, beneath the green,
With jokes and jests, life's a big scene.
In nature's arms, we find our bliss,
Sharing giggles, we can't miss.

## **Whispers of the Fruiting Trees**

The trees sigh secrets in gentle tones,
Berries gossip, and laughter moans.
Each fruit has a tale, a chuckle to share,
As leaves quiver, we breathe in the air.

A pear slips down with a giggle so bold,
Its juicy punch, like stories told.
While cherries tease, all dressed in red,
They giggle softly, "Come join our spread!"

With zestful zests, they pop and burst,
Creating giggles, oh how they thirst!
For every bite is an echo so bright,
We munch and laugh from morning to night.

Beneath fruit-laden boughs, we weave our cheer,
In nature's theater, the world feels near.
With silly faces and playful schemes,
We find ourselves lost in luscious dreams.

## A Journey Through Green

Through tangled paths, we set our feet,
With gooey snacks, our jokes repeat.
Bouncing over roots and dappled light,
Each step sends us into pure delight.

The weather's warm, it calls for fun,
A runaway grape makes us all run!
Chasing giggles, a fruity chase,
Each berry kingdom, our silly space.

With belly laughs floating on the breeze,
We play tag with squirrels hiding in trees.
Loopy voices echo as we play,
In nature's playground, we brightly sway.

The vibrant hues paint our joyful spree,
In delightful chaos, oh can't you see?
With every turn, we gain a new sound,
In laughter's embrace, we joyfully bound.

## The Harvest's Quiet Whispers


Amidst the leaves a secret hum,
The apples laugh, the peaches drum.
'Hey, pick me first!' they seem to cry,
While pears are playing hide and sly.

Grapes are gossiping on the vine,
'Did you see the squash? It crossed the line!'
Pumpkins roll and give a cheer,
As carrots wink from cover near.

The tomatoes blush, they're feeling grand,
As zucchinis try to form a band.
'Let's have a dance beneath the sun,'
The harvest says, 'Oh, let's have fun!'

So gather 'round, both fruit and seed,
In nature's jest, we plant the seed.
A quirky crew in shades of green,
In laughter lies the harvest's sheen.

## Sanctum of Sheltered Souls.

In the grassy nook, where shadows play,
The veggies plot their wild ballet.
Carrots wear shades, they think they're cool,
While onions giggle, breaking the rule.

Beans climb high to reach the sky,
'Let's have a feast, oh my, oh my!'
Cabbages roll and twirl around,
In this small world where joy is found.

Squash tell tales of grandest dreams,
While radishes whisper in snickering schemes.
The lettuce waltzes, soft and spry,
In the rhythm of breezes that softly sigh.

So come gather here, friends come and greet,
In this silly space, life is a treat.
With every chuckle and hearty cheer,
In our leafy home, nothing to fear.

## Fruits of Solitude

Up in the boughs, where plumpness grows,
Fruits play hide and seek, nobody knows.
'Citrus twisties, come out and play!'
'We're busy juicing,' they giggle away.

Berries huddle in cozy clumps,
Sharing secrets and funny thumps.
'Did you hear what the melon said?
He rolled away, and that's how he fled!'

The bananas tease and goof about,
'Let's form a band, with a rhythmic shout!'
The cherries jive, all shiny bright,
In cozy corners, they dance with light.

In this lone garden, where laughter blooms,
Fruits spread joy and fill the rooms.
Come join the fun, don't stay aloof,
In the world of whimsy, there's always proof.

## Whispers in the Grove

In a hidden grove where giggles rise,
The fruits conspire, oh what a surprise!
Cherries chuckle, 'Look at that pear!'
'He's stuck in the branch, oh we must care!'

Apples gossip, sliding on dew,
'What's with the prune? He's feeling blue!'
While berries bounce in the gentle breeze,
Teasing each other with nimble ease.

The nuts are cracking jokes galore,
'Let's roll away and find some more!'
Lemons are grinning in tangy cheer,
'Life's zesty here, come join us dear!'

So roam the paths where laughter flows,
In this fruity world, anything goes.
With each playful whiff, and every muse,
The grove's invisible joy, we choose.

## Fruitful Reveries

In the green hall of apples, they dance,
A pear in a tux, giving chance a glance.
Peaches in laughter, they burst with glee,
As cherries joke, 'Come hang out with me!'

Bananas slip past, a slippery race,
While grapes gossip softly, a round little face.
Lemons jump in, adding zest to the show,
'Hope you like sour,' they cheekily crow.

A fig in a hat tells the strangest tales,
Joking with berries, the laughter prevails.
Fruits all around, a whimsical spree,
In this merry garden, so full of glee!

With violets giggling, the laughter grows loud,
As fruits flaunt their colors, so vibrant and proud.
In a world of sheer joy, where laughter's the tune,
The orchard's alive, dancing under the moon!

## The Embrace of Flora

A daisy wore sneakers, it loved to jog,
While tulips did yoga, a real clever smog.
Roses tucked in, all snug in their beds,
And sunflowers giggled, stroking their heads.

Dandelions whispered their wildest dreams,
Sharing their secrets in soft little schemes.
The petunias pranced in a colorful line,
With laughter so loud, they changed every sign.

Snapdragons grinned wide, as they told tall tales,
While lilies played cards, ignoring the gales.
Oh, what a meadow of laughter and fun,
Where flora embraces, under the sun!

Each blossom's a heartbeat, a comical sound,
In nature's grand circus, bright joy can be found.
They twirl and they leap, under skies so blue,
In the embrace of flora, laughter is true!

## **Nightfall in the Orchard**

When the stars come to play, the fruit takes a nap,
A cherry tells stories from under its cap.
The moon giggles softly, draping beams all around,
As pears in pajamas begin to abound.

A raccoon in glasses reads tales to the night,
While figs hold their breath—hoping things turn out right.
The owls start to hoot, while the apples eat cake,
As memories dance, from the fruit they awake.

Plums tell the jokes — they're no fruity old prunes,
Bananas slip past, like whimsical tunes.
In this twilight garden, where laughter's enshrined,
The night wraps its arms, holding joy intertwined.

With shadows that tumble, and crickets that sing,
They celebrate together, the happiness spring.
As the night softly whispers, in dreamy delight,
The orchard is laughing, embracing the night!

## Sonnet of the Sunlit Grove

In the grove, where sunshine tickles each leaf,
A lime told a lime, 'We're the best of reprieve!'
Mangoes boasted, 'We can dance and sway,'
While apples chimed in, 'But we're here to stay!'

Nuts were all cracking up, stirring the ground,
While flowers grew brighter, their laughter unbound.
Each berry a comedian, ripe with a jest,
The joy in this grove makes the heart feel blessed.

With wind as the stagehand, the orchard's alive,
As fruit comes together, they giggle and strive.
In this sunlit ballet, with nature's own rhyme,
The grove hums the songs of good laughter and time.

So gather, my friends, under bright sunny beams,
Join the merry chorus, where fruit dances with dreams.
In this vibrant escape, find laughter your guide,
In the sonnet of joy, let your spirits abide!

## The Lullaby of the Branches

In a tree with a dream so sweet,
The squirrels dance on tiny feet.
Bouncing berries like little balls,
They giggle and tease as autumn calls.

Crickets sing tunes of silly flings,
As the branches sway and play with springs.
A sleepy owl hoots in delight,
Waving goodnight to the stars so bright.

The leaves rustle in a laughing spree,
Whispering jokes as fresh as can be.
With a lullaby wrapped in green,
The tree sways with joy, a merry scene.

So rest your head on mossy beds,
Dream of acorns and sleepy threads.
For in this grove, laughter abounds,
With every giggle in leafy sounds.

## **Where Petals Drift and Dreams Blossom**


Petals tumble down with a frolicsome twirl,
Inviting the bees to join in their whirl.
They giggle and dance in a floral parade,
Turning the garden into a jesters' glade.

A sunflower frowns, feeling quite tall,
While daisies tease, 'You're just one and all!'
With blossoms in bloom, the air's filled with jest,
Where laughter and nectar mingle in zest.

In the shade of the tree, a picnic unfolds,
With sandwiches wearing their mustard golds.
The ants strip the crumbs like they're meant for a feast,
While a ladybug winks, a confetti beast.

So come and join where the petals do sway,
In the garden of glee, come and play, play, play!
For in every bloom, a chuckle is sewn,
Where joy and absurdity brightly are grown.

## Secrets Shared with the Wind

The wind spins tales with a snicker and sigh,
Catching the secrets that drift and fly.
Leaves whisper laughter, a rustling glee,
Bringing wild stories for you and me.

A ladybug's party, oh what a delight,
Dancing in circles under moonlight bright.
With emotions burst forth like bubbles in air,
The wind tickles each blossom with playful care.

A kite gets tangled in a branch's charm,
While the squirrels chuckle, they mean no harm.
With every gust, a chuckle escapes,
A symphony born from nature's shapes.

So listen closely to the breezy cheer,
In the whispers of the wind, the fun is clear.
For secrets abound where laughter's the tune,
And every rustle feels like a boon.

## Mysteries of the Verdant Realm


Beneath the boughs where secrets play,
Frogs recite poems in a croaky way.
Mushrooms wear hats, quite dapper and fine,
As whispers of mischief dance on the vine.

The rabbits hold meetings to scheme and plot,
Over carrots and snacks they've just got.
A raccoon's a bandit, but oh what a show,
Stealing the snacks, saying 'Just let it go!'

Every nook has a tale to spread,
Of quirky encounters where laughter led.
The deer in the dawn get tickled by grass,
As giggles and snorts make the moments pass.

So wander these woods with a light-hearted glance,
Join in the tales of the critters' dance.
In the realm of green where the funny takes flight,
Every leaf tells a story, each day and each night.

www.ingramcontent.com/pod-product-compliance
Lightning Source LLC
Chambersburg PA
CBHW060145230426
43661CB00003B/574